REGIONAL LANDSCAPE ARCHITECTURE
Northern California

Rooted in Resilience

JEFFREY HEAD

SCHIFFER PUBLISHING

4880 Lower Valley Road • Atglen, PA 19310

Other Schiffer Books by Jeffrey Head:

Regional Landscape Architecture: Southern California,
ISBN 978-0-7643-5836-4

Other Schiffer Books on Related Subjects:

Designing for Disaster: Domestic Architecture in the Era of Climate Change,
Boyce Thompson, 978-0-7643-5784-8

Anatomy of a Great Home, Boyce Thompson, ISBN 978-0-7643-5465-6

Designed by Ashley Millhouse
Cover design by Brenda McCallum
Front cover photo: Art Gray
Back cover photo: Marion Brenner
Type set in ZapfHumnst BT/ZapfEllipt BT

ISBN: 978-0-7643-5835-7
Printed in China

Published by Schiffer Publishing, Ltd.
4880 Lower Valley Road
Atglen, PA 19310
Phone: (610) 593-1777; Fax: (610) 593-2002
E-mail: Info@schifferbooks.com
Web: www.schifferbooks.com

For our complete selection of fine books on this and related subjects, please visit our website at www.schifferbooks.com. You may also write for a free catalog. Schiffer Publishing's titles are available at special discounts for bulk purchases for sales promotions or premiums. Special editions, including personalized covers, corporate imprints, and excerpts, can be created in large quantities for special needs. For more information, contact the publisher.
We are always looking for people to write books on new and related subjects. If you have an idea for a book, please contact us at proposals@schifferbooks.com.

CONTENTS

FOREWORD

Thirty or so years ago, Big Sur architect Mickey Muening, whom I revere to a mythical status, asked my husband, ecologist and designer Paul Kephart, to re-create the surrounding meadows on the rooftops of new bungalows at the now-famous Post Ranch Inn. As the story goes, what began as a lighthearted quest to evoke appreciation of the coastline's natural beauty sparked Paul's obsessive pursuit to craft landscapes, buildings, and systems that adapt and thrive—what is now known as "living architecture."

These postage stamp–sized rooftop meadows led him down the path of scientific inquisition, of re-creating the exact plant ecology of a disappearing native coastal grassland. It evolved as a quest to promote species diversity—plants at first, and then, because nothing in nature stands alone, to attract the creatures who relied on and benefited from those plants. The insects, pollinators, birds, creatures, and humans who found themselves hemmed in by development were given relief, areas of respite. I like to think that, somewhat intuitively, the vision became to create habitat corridors in areas increasingly dotted with concrete and glass.

Realizing this pursuit required the estalishment plant-growing facilities that could supply native, water-wise, and drought-tolerant vegetation, which is a dizzying and specialized endeavor. Breeding, selection, and propagation of these kinds of plants continues to be passed down to new generations of nursery managers and the clients and aficionados who support it.

In the landscape there is always more than meets the eye. The many layers beneath the vegetation became the next foray. On rooftops particularly, it included coming to understand the natural process of hydrology, optimizing soil health and performance, and the development of products that enhance the longevity of the design and ease of delivery.

Further collaboration to encourage municipalities to reward living architecture projects turned the trend into a viable standard for modern building. Our water, energy, and waste are renewable and reusable, and when living systems are integrated into the built environment, we all benefit.

What began as a search for beauty, enhancement, and adornment has led to a complementary scientific pursuit. At Raina Creek Design, this journey has been defined not by a storyline of good versus bad, or of overcoming, but by the process of discovery that allows for adaptation and adjustment. We now know, for example, that humans heal 30 percent faster when exposed to even a photograph of nature. And that in all projects we design, we can harvest and collect more water than we need for irrigation, eliminating the practice of using our precious potable water for nonpotable uses. We know how much carbon plants and soil can sequester and how to enhance carbon storage in the soil. Even solar photovoltaic (PV) performance is enhanced when placed on top of vegetation such as a green roof. We've learned how to grow large landscapes without artificial fertilizers and pesticides, and this in turn is applicable to large-scale food production.

Our collective capacity for adaptation is what drives our excitement for the future. Overpopulation, resource scarcity, pollution, and climate change are certain realities today. Our focus now, and that of many of our peers, is to accelerate the adoption and scalability of

living architecture and its systems and technologies.

Our residential designs consider site, context, and its capacity for all of these ecological functions—that's the science part. The art is to design it in a way that is beautiful, reflects our values, and makes us feel good. There is a joyous aspect to what we do, and it's fun, and it's a constant exploration and discovery of our interpretation of beauty.

For us, the development of these principles began in residential Northern California landscapes— our first living, evolving laboratories. Because of supportive people with shared values and principles, we are now sharing a better future for all creatures. We hope that this book reinforces the vision for an ecological design approach that enhances our lives and communities and goes beyond sustainability.

May the language of ecology and landscape quench our appetite for beauty and remind us why, with enthusiasm and joy, we choose to pursue art, science, architecture, and design. This is and always will be a worthwhile endeavor—to celebrate a vibrant future for all.

—Marta Kephart

Vice President and COO

INTRODUCTION

I became interested in landscape architecture as a result of my research into modernism and modern design. Twenty-five years ago I happened upon the names of California's best-known postwar-era landscape architects: Thomas Church, Garrett Eckbo, and Lawrence Halprin. I had read Eckbo's *Landscape for Living*, Church's *Gardens Are for People: How to Plan for Outdoor Living*, and writings by Lawrence Halprin, especially his Letter to the Editor published in *House Beautiful* (May 1948), which I find to be the most insightful of his writings. Although each had a different perspective and approach, collectively they represented the foundations of modern landscape architecture in California.

Recently I reread these books in the sitting area of my own garden. Their notions about space, environment, and experience were ground-breaking for their time, but they are just as relevant today. The work of Church, Eckbo, and Halprin and their peers has become part of our regional vernacular.

"California is such a different place than the rest of the country in terms of culture, and more than that, in terms of climate and ecology," says landscape architect Laura Jerrard of Lutsko Associates Landscape, who also lectures in Eckbo's former department, the College of Environmental Design at UC Berkeley. "I think those landscape architects acknowledged that in their way, and landscape architects working here today continue to do so, maybe taking tangents but building on that pioneering spirit."

Alain Peauroi, owner of the landscape architecture firm Terremoto, agrees. "Tommy [Church] kind of set the foundation for residential design in Northern California. He used natural elements and did not do too many crazy, fancy things; he just worked with what the existing site had and maximized on that . . . which is something we try to do in our work."

Jennifer Ivanovich of BaDesign also acknowledges Eckbo's influence: "When I was in graduate school, I had the opportunity to work on Garrett Eckbo's former home in the Berkeley Hills," she says. "That was my introduction to his style, which is modest, comfortable, and modern, but not severe. His structural use of plants and his social motivations are admirable."

The projects in this book share those values. With their attention to environment and site, materials, water use, lighting, and low maintenance, they explore what it means to have a regionally appropriate garden. The designs also reflect social habits such as the indoor-outdoor living for which California is known. As Halprin wrote, "A good garden is one which fulfills best the needs of the people who live in it."[1]

While the entire state is a temperate zone, Northern California's climate is different from Southern California's. Coastal fog and proximity to the Sierra Mountains contribute to Northern California's precipitation and access to water, compared to Southern California's arid climate. Northern California also has more microclimates and soil types and a wider temperature range.

Regardless of region, aesthetics is a key component of any landscape design, whose deeper purpose is to connect humans emotionally with the land. Halprin wrote that "the great challenge for the garden designer is not to make the garden look natural but to make the garden so the people in it will feel natural."[2] Eckbo said it this way: "Our major objective is the integration, the harmonization, the coordination of, or the establishment of good relations between the physical forms of nature and the physical manifestations of man in the landscape."[3]

The projects in this book make deliberate use of borrowed landscape, or Church's "theory of visual appropriation."[4] This is the notion that one's immediate landscape can be enriched by framing a distant view or feature of a neighboring garden. They also relate directly to the buildings around them, sometimes blurring the boundaries. "Planting is intended to enhance architecture, not hide or compete with it,"[5] Church wrote.

Indeed, landscape architects are trained to treat buildings and the land as one canvas. Sarah Kuehl of Einwiller Kuehl sees design as an opportunity "to work collaboratively with the architecture and the site to make a landscape which is more than the sum of its parts." In the 1950s, Eckbo said that "the sensitive landscape architect finds himself impelled to carry on with some extension of structure into the garden. Conversely the modern architect felt himself impelled to bring the garden into the house with plants and glass, rock and water."[6]

A garden is an invitation to engage, to participate in the dynamic experience of living with nature's ecosystems, and a regionally attuned garden sustains us environmentally, emotionally, psychologically, and physically.

"In California we have such a strong and specific connection to the history of architectural modernism in that we have always identified the potential to live outside," says Roderick Wyllie of Surfacedesign. "But how that has been expressed in terms of landscape architecture was, I think, sometimes a bit too literally connected to the architecture. In my mind that conversation has opened up a bit." The following projects are part of this expanding perspective.

1. Lawrence Halprin, "How Far Can Naturalism Go in a Garden?," *House Beautiful*, May 1948, 163.

2. Ibid., 164.

3. Garrett Eckbo, *Landscape for Living* (New York: Dodge, 1950), 38.

4. Thomas Dolliver Church, *Gardens Are for People: How to Plan for Outdoor Living* (New York: Reinhold, 1955), 27.

5. Ibid., 38.

6. Eckbo, *Landscape for Living*, 75.

PALO ALTO GARDEN

PALO ALTO
BADESIGN

"There is a difference
between watering a
lawn when all you are
doing is stepping on
it, and using water to
feed yourselves and
your neighbors."

—*JENNIFER IVANOVICH*

Previous page:
A living fence supports pixie mandarins, one of several citrus plants growing on the fan-shaped steel espalier.

This page:
Along the side yard, a slim cedar deck sits flush with the kitchen floor, and potted herbs are within easy reach. BaDesign fabricated the yellow powder-coated steel stools. *Photos: Branden Adams / BaDesign, except where noted*

Decorative river rock along the fence is an alternative to mulch and acts as a weed barrier. A trellis screens the neighbor's driveway.
Photo: Keith Baker

Originally the first post office in Palo Alto, this converted house was moved to its current downtown location in the late 1890s. The long, slender 1,500-square-foot dwelling and its 2,600-square-foot lot are considered small by today's standards.

After living in San Francisco for a few years, the owners returned to Palo Alto and began a house remodel that included transforming the landscape into a hearty edible garden. Except for existing plum, apricot, and peach trees, the yard was mostly grass and dirt.

"The husband is what I call an intense fruitavore. He really loves fruit and wanted all these different varieties," says landscape architect Jennifer Ivanovich. "The wife, an architect, did not want the garden to be too crazy. She wanted the landscaping and planting to be clean and modern."

With her background in conservation biology and ecology, Ivanovich welcomed the opportunity to balance their respective desires. Having a large selection of edibles would offer both utility and an immediate connection with the landscape.

"I created something that was not visually noisy but still had lots of variety," Ivanovich says.

Almost every part of the property was pressed into service. Its key component is a Corten steel–framed fruit tree espalier near the street that forms a screen between the house and the neighbor's driveway. It contains fifteen kinds of fruit arranged in an alternating pattern of citrus with other fruits.

All metalwork, including the espalier, was custom designed and fabricated in the firm's shop. The use of Corten for the entry gate, trash enclosure, and planters creates a cohesive aesthetic. "The Corten elements give the project uniformity and tone down the cacophony of the various things going on," Ivanovich says.

The landscape includes nearly fifty types of fruits and herbs. Next to the espalier, vegetables and herbs sprout from two planter boxes, and more planter boxes and fruiting shrubs and trees—from Meyer lemon to currant, persimmon, and fig, to name a few—are tucked in along the edges of this narrow property. Pawpaw trees were added during the installation when the client learned they can be grown in this region. This was an exciting prospect since he grew up eating the tree's custard-like fruit in Pennsylvania.

Seasonal greens are contained in Corten steel planters with friendly rolled edges fabricated by BaDesign. Concrete pavers offer a transition from the decomposed granite to the wood steps and decking at the front of the house.

A powder-coated yellow
swinging light armature by
BaDesign illuminates the
activity area.
Photo: Keith Baker

BaDesign custom-made most of the light fixtures, too, lending this hard-working garden an air of refinement. Uplights highlight the espalier fence, a small spotlight focuses on the pineapple guava tree in the front yard, and small path lights illuminate the pawpaw trees along the side of the house. In the backyard are two swinging armatures with lights, one in the sitting area and the other near the barbecue. At the back of the garden, trellising provides a structure for lighting a small lawn that was later replaced with decomposed granite to conserve water.

Although this is not a drought-tolerant landscape, "there is a difference between watering a lawn when all you are doing is stepping on it, and using water to feed yourselves and your neighbors," Ivanovich says. (See site plan for partial plant list.)

This project led BaDesign to produce a modern, customizable edibles kit consisting of metal-crafted components including trellises, planters, compost bins, and armatures such as tomato cages, which can also be treated as garden sculpture.

Pea plants climb one of several steel vegetable armatures fabricated by BaDesign. The U-channel trellising provides support and allows light through the structure.

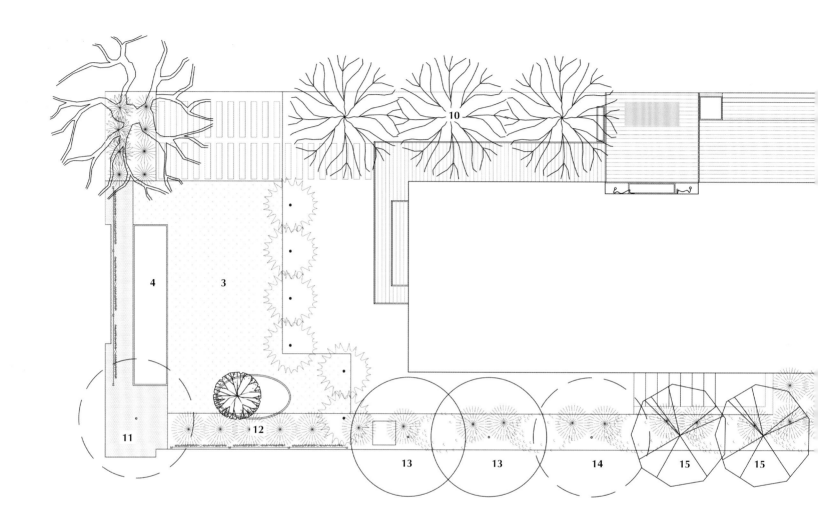

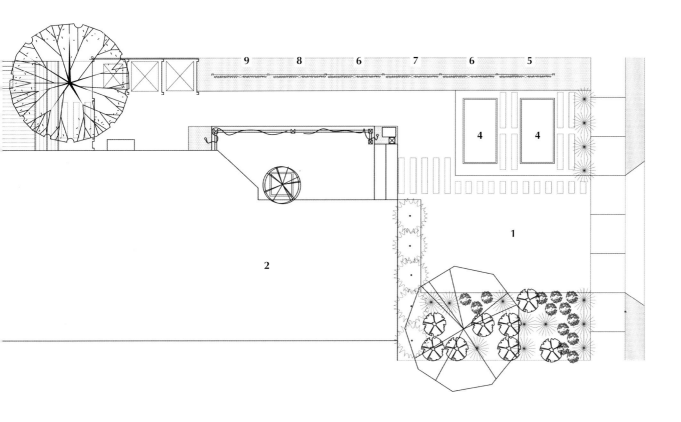

1	Driveway	**6**	4-in-1 Asian pear	**11**	Apricot
2	House	**7**	Pixie mandarin	**12**	Concord and Niagara grapes
3	Lawn	**8**	Tarocco blood orange	**13**	Plum
4	Seasonal herbs and vegetables	**9**	4-in-1 cherry	**14**	Peach
5	Bearss lime	**10**	Fuji persimmon	**15**	Paw-paw

URBAN SPRING

SAN FRANCISCO
BIONIC

"We've abandoned some plant choices because others have been more adaptable to the situation. It is not a fussy planting design; we like a rough look to the garden."

—MARCEL WILSON

Prevous page:
Views from the deck show the boardwalk and diagonal stair to the sundeck and lawn. Water from a rain chain and natural spring flows through runnels to the basin and into a wetland at the property's lowest point. *Photos: Marion Brenner*

Clematis vines and western red cedar screens provide varying transparencies at the property's edges. Irises bloom in the wetland.

After a lengthy search for a property that could become a "project," Bionic design director Marcel Wilson and his wife found a half-renovated house with a neglected backyard containing dead trees and struggling plants. "We said, 'Perfect!'" Wilson recalls.

Its unusual feature is a groundwater spring with artesian pressure near the back steps that yields more than a hundred gallons a day. The flow, about the diameter of a pencil, is consistent throughout the year and was a source of backyard flooding—but also inspired Wilson's design concept.

"It's an unusual geotechnical condition," he says. "Veins of clay run in the soil and make seeps." Sometimes referred to as nuisance water, it typically goes into a drain and gets pumped into the sewer. Wilson intended to put it to use before letting it soak back into the ground.

For two years Wilson watched and measured the activity before developing a design for the 25-by-50-foot yard. He found many different growing conditions, which is unusual in a small garden: loamy and clay soils, full sun and full shade, and both saturated and dry areas.

The underground spring largely defined the garden's layout and character. Wilson captured the bubbling water in a stone-filled basin and a series of runnels that direct water to the lowest part of the garden. Wood pathways allow the garden to be viewed and tended from different vantage points, and the garden's strong diagonals offer a dynamic counterpoint to the growth patterns, shapes, and colors of the plantings, especially when viewed from the house's first- and second-floor decks. The gentle flow of water through the runnels makes a rhythmic sound that can also be heard in the house.

New building materials from the house renovation were brought into the garden. Steel from the seismic upgrade reappears as outdoor staircase stringers and on some of the deck framing. Ipe wood off-cuts from the upper decking became stair treads. And dirt from the basement excavation was used to backfill a new garden wall. Since there is no access on the sides of the house, everything was hauled to the backyard through the house—soil, trees, steel, and debris.

At left, a copper rain chain channels rainwater into the spring basin under the canopy of a Sango-kaku Japanese maple and woodland plants. Decking provides service access through the garden.

The lower runnel flows into a painted steel-frame box filled with black Mexican pebbles. Water from the steel box dissipates into the wetland, providing irrigation and wildlife habitat.

The upper runnel flows into the copper water box, lending a pleasant sensory experience to the space. A miniature deck, watercress, Japanese bloodgrass, mondo grass, and Mexican pebbles surround the water box.

Wilson is intrigued by the performance of two vine maple trees he planted next to the spring. "One of them is planted in part sun in loam soil that is not saturated," he says. "The other tree, planted 5 or 6 feet away, has a different cycle of budding, leafing, and changing color." The design also borrows a view of a neighbor's cabbage tree and corkscrew willows on the downhill side of the property.

He stocked the garden with a Sango-kaku Japanese maple and other maple trees, Japanese blood grass, Douglas iris, Louisiana iris, bamboo, four types of ferns, and a redwood sorrel tree whose leaves look like giant four-leaf clovers. A tea tree was one of the few original plantings to survive decades of wet soil.

The house provides ambient light to the landscape, so outdoor lighting consists of only a few uplights. "We just wanted lighting to enhance the composition of the yard; it felt right to not make it bright," Wilson says.

Maintenance consists simply of cutting back growth twice a year. The garden is an ongoing work in progress as Wilson finesses the design around the site's peculiarities. "We've abandoned some plant choices because others have been more adaptable to the situation," he says. "It is not a fussy planting design; we like a rough look to the garden."

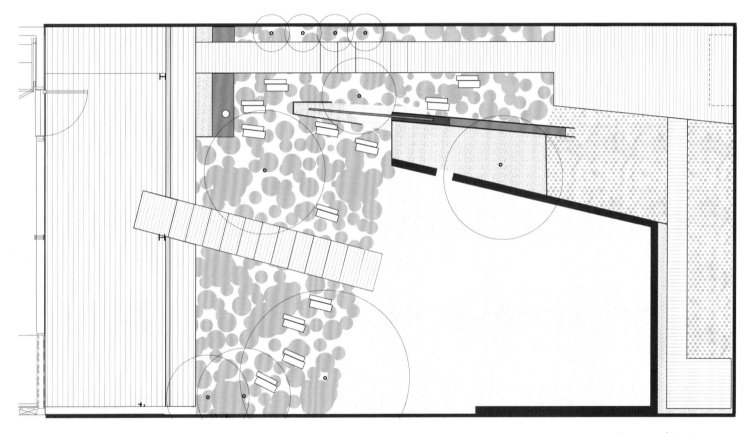

Courtesy of Bionic

FIVE RIDGE FARM

SANTA ROSA
BIONIC

"Beauty is important, but what the landscape can do is just as important as how it looks."

—*MARCEL WILSON*

Previous page:
A stair landing in the cutting garden parallels the site's sloping contours. Mild-steel edges and walls lead to shade under large oak trees. *Photos: Marion Brenner*

Terraced cutting gardens in summer.

This somewhat remote, off-the-grid property is set on 60 acres in the Mayacama Mountains north of Santa Rosa. It survived the area's devastating 2017 firestorm even though flames came within hundreds of feet of the site. For the owners, an environmental attorney and an organic farmer, fire resistance was a priority in the property's development. A solar array generates all their electricity, and water is extracted from a well linked to two large water tanks.

The design was a collaboration between landscape architect Marcel Wilson and architect David Huan, who designed the house. A zigzag system of paths leads from the loop road to the house and pool, which also functions as a firefighting reservoir. Those paths serve a dual purpose as a fireline and walkway. Decomposed granite, edged with ½-inch mild steel, makes for a gentle walk up the slope to the house. The path leads to a shady area and a vegetable garden on the house's south side. In the full-sun garden, a foil to the nearby oak woodland, Wilson planted yarrow, discaria, poppies, Penta sedums, and euphorbias. The few irrigated areas orient visitors to the front of the house.

Meadow grasses, which turn green in winter, surround the steel pathways that traverse the slope and create a firebreak.

A mild-steel screen hides farm equipment.

A lap pool doubles as a fire reservoir.

Its location some distance from the road meant that heavy earthwork machinery disturbed some of the soils during construction. Grassland root systems were remedied to improve growth and drainage. Wilson also aerated and decompacted the ground around the affected oaks to get air to their roots. The grasslands were then reseeded with a native grass mix.

Landscape lighting is minimal and far below the limits outlined in the Sonoma County Dark Sky Ordinance. LED lighting was installed around the house and in the pool. Otherwise, as Wilson says, "If you need a light, you get a flashlight."

Low maintenance and drought tolerance take on new meaning in this remote area. The mostly drought-tolerant plantings eliminate the need

for water, and the perennials' natural cycle of decay and decomposition supplies all the nutrients the plants need. "It takes five years, I think, for a landscape to establish its cycles and gain some balance," Wilson says. In this self-regulating landscape, removing downed branches, redressing pathways with decomposed granite, keeping the tall grass short during the fire season, and minimal irrigation are the ongoing requirements.

The absence of a recognizable style reflects Wilson's holistic approach. "I am always trying to make our work do more than just be pretty," he says. "Beauty is important, but what the landscape can do is just as interesting to me as how it looks."

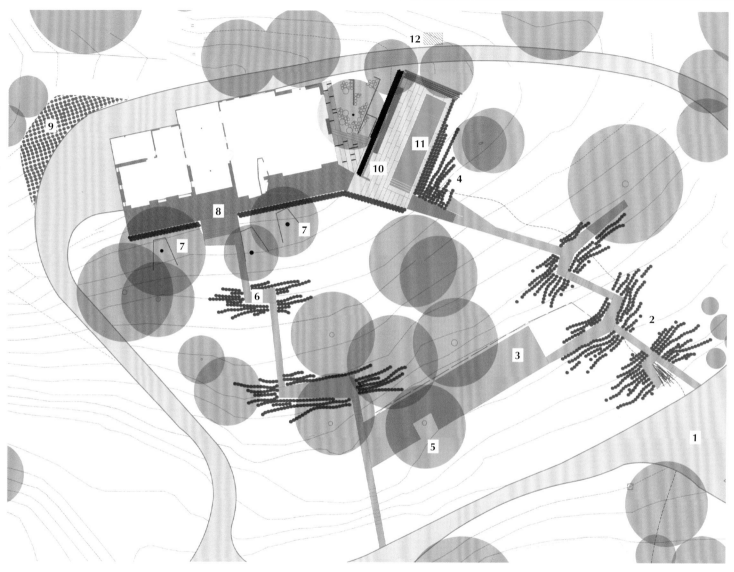

Courtesy of Bionic

1	Loop road	5	Existing oaks	9	Fire tanks
2	Cutting gardens	6	Landings	10	Bench
3	Terrace	7	Tree wells	11	Pool/fire reservoir
4	Stairs	8	Deck	12	Equipment screen

CALISTOGA GARDEN

CALISTOGA
EINWILLER KUEHL

"The plan connects
and divides elements
to draw the eye
toward long and short
views that integrate
these multiple scales
of space and garden."

—SARAH KUEHL

Previous page: Existing elements such as the walnut trees, water tower, and swimming pool were composed into a simple garden organized by a linear stone wall and path. *Photos: Nic Lehoux, except where noted*

Seating was inserted beneath the sheltering canopy of two large walnut trees, with direct views to the vineyards.

The walnut garden viewed
from the vineyard.

When the owners of a boutique vineyard contacted Einwiller Kuehl about a landscape redesign, reducing water use was at the top of their wish list. They also wanted to preserve two large walnut trees, a water tower, and a swimming pool, while creating a better flow of outdoor space.

Einwiller Kuehl developed a functional, intuitive plan that uses the setting to great effect. "We wanted to create a connection to the surrounding landscapes, which act as containers for the garden—first the mountains that frame the valley, then the vineyards that create an expanse of agricultural landscape, then the site's buildings, and lastly, the interior spaces of the house," says firm cofounder Sarah Kuehl. The plan connects and divides elements "to draw the eye away, toward long and short views that integrate these multiple scales of space and garden," she says.

Three new gardens—an entry court, oasis garden, and walnut terrace—are linked by a linear stone wall and path. "This stone gesture is a continuation of the surrounding vineyard rows, stepping in height from path to wall to bench to serving counter based on one's vantage point in the garden," Kuehl says.

On approach, an olive tree allée aligns with the vineyard's geometry and leads to a gravel court, which doubles as a formal arrival area and tractor entry to the vineyard during the harvest crush. A Mediterranean palette of agaves and native grasses and a dwarf olive hedge is planted near the front porch, which wraps around three sides of the house to offer views to the north, south, and east. The largest deck area outside the kitchen and living area overlooks the oasis garden.

Zoning is key to smart water management. "We gathered all of the 'wet' elements—the pool, a lawn, and water-loving plants—into one area to celebrate the cool wetness in an oasis," Kuehl

A gravel court functions as a parking area and supports agricultural programs such as the annual grape crush. Simple low-water plantings—agaves, maiden grass, and a dwarf olive hedge—define an elegant entry into the family home.

The existing buildings were set into new gardens, with views that connect to the mountains and agricultural valley floor.
Photo: Matthew Millman

explains. "The remaining garden areas contain low-water plants, and gravel is an important part of the design." In the old scheme, pavement surrounded the pool; now its small border of lawn offers lush relief from the heat and the drier areas.

On the walnut terrace at the back of the house, a seating area beneath the canopy of two monumental walnut trees provides views of the Napa Valley hills, and a nearby bocce court is another source of family enjoyment.

Einwiller Kuehl collaborated closely with the architects to align planting compositions with large windows. "We created numerous elegant and perfectly framed views on all sides of the home," Kuehl says. "There are long axial views, formal agrarian compositions, and abstract greenery, which transforms the interior of the home and makes the landscape significant both inside and outside."

To respect the agricultural valley and the rural darkness, landscape lighting is kept to a minimum. Only the pool and stairs are lit, aside from downlights on the two walnut trees.

"Gardens are living things and need tending and even plant replacement over time," Kuehl says, "but the plants selected and the anticipated maintenance here suggest a very long life."

The front porch was expanded into a large deck and wraps around three sides of the home, providing functional terraces with views facing north, south, and east.
Photo: Matthew Millman

A lawn oasis surrounds the pool, previously hemmed in by paveament. *Photo: Matthew Millman*

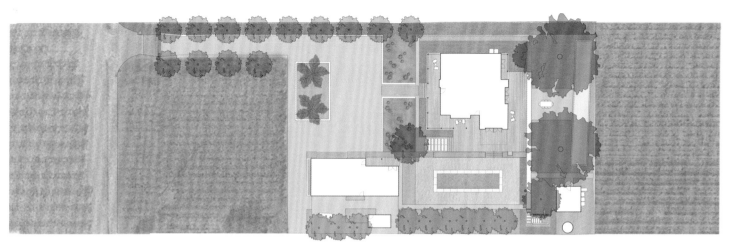

Courtesy of Einwiller Kuehl

Courtesy of Einwiller Kuehl

ORINDA GARDEN

ORINDA
KSA DESIGN STUDIO

"Once all the plants
are established we
look at creating a story
or a theme with the
lighting and create a
hierarchy."

—*JAKE PATTON*

Previous page:
The entry drive is set between a newly planted vineyard and a rose garden. *Photos: Steve Lacap*

Nearly a third of the site is reserved for a garden that provides year-round vegetables for the family.

A visual axis links the house, pool, and pool house.

After remodeling their home, the owners turned their attention to the landscape, which they asked KSA to design in phases. The formerly underused landscape, dotted with mature live oaks, redwoods, and sycamores, now contains discrete spaces that draw the owners out into nature.

KSA principals Katherine Spitz and Jake Patton first designed a motor court with a water feature, a small vineyard for family use, and a deck outside the master suite to improve access to a new outdoor spa. Then came a koi pond, followed by a zero-edge pool and pool house that act as the backyard's centerpiece and organizing feature. These new areas are connected by pathways and gardens with native and adapted plantings, including trees such as valley oak, western redbud, and vine hill manzanita, and shrubs such as California wood fern, sage, and rosemary. The lawn areas contain buffalo and St. Augustine turfgrass.

At the back of the property, a 4-foot retaining wall pushes back the hillside, which added about 12 feet of flat area for a bocce court. Much of the cut-and-fill soil was retained on site, which reduced construction costs, although the soil had to be heavily amended for plantings. Drought-tolerant buffalo and blue grama grasses were planted around the bocce ball court, and the carpet geranium and Johnson's Blue geranium ground covers throughout the landscape were chosen for their low maintenance.

Stone-clad, raised vegetable beds aid irrigation and drainage. Measuring about 20 inches high by 15 feet long, they were scaled to be a comfortable height and depth to work in without back strain.

Patton estimates there are close to 300 light fixtures on the grounds. "Once all the plants are established we look at creating a story or a theme with the lighting and create a hierarchy," he says. To avoid under- or overlighting the landscape, Patton met with the owners to identify the signature elements and how to highlight them for nighttime. Since many areas are in use at night, there was a need for safety and security, as well as ambiance.

A path leads to the koi pond and up the hill, adding another vista and creating the illusion of greater space.

"We did a series of different types of low-voltage lighting fixtures, such as a wall wash with LEDs; halogen Step Star low-profile lights for the motor court, which illuminate the area out to the sides; and LED strip lights for the pedestrian paths," he says. "Uplights were placed in the pool area for dramatic effect. And in the koi pond, the owners requested RGB lights for a playful and colorful effect. These lights can be adjusted to different colors or set to automatically change color."

He adds, "The owners now spend more than half their time outside when the weather is good. It has changed their lifestyle,"

Although the cultivated landscape is considerably larger now, the use of drought-tolerant and native plantings keeps maintenance and costs manageable. A smart irrigation system, which interacts with weather and moisture sensors, consists of drip irrigation in the planted beds and efficient rotator spray nozzles for the small parcels of lawn.

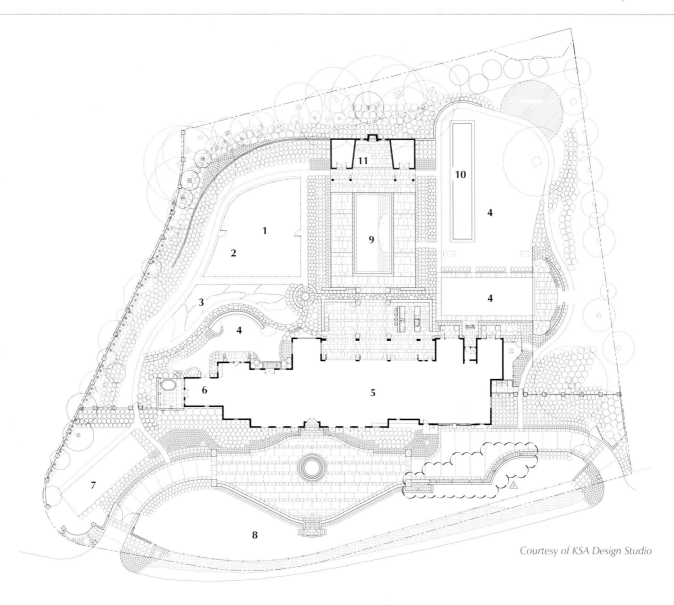

Courtesy of KSA Design Studio

1	Vegetable gardens	6	Master bath and outdoor spa
2	Chicken coop	7	Bus pad
3	Cutting garden	8	Vineyard
4	Lawn	9	Pool
5	House	10	Bocce court

NAPA GARDEN

ST. HELENA
LUTSKO ASSOCIATES

The house was sited
for optimal views of
the vineyards and
mountains, which was
important to give it a
sense of place.

Previous page:
Rectilinear stepping stones
bridge the playful
perennials and terminate
at the pool terrace. A
mature oak frames the
pool house and references
the hillside oaks beyond.
Photos: Art Gray

Linear bands of perennials
and grasses stretch out to
the surrounding vineyard.
Rows of vines echo the
pattern at a distance.

A nod to the farmland, rustic materials such as wood and concrete take contemporary, minimalist forms.

Set on 4 acres in the Napa Valley's Rutherford wine region, this second home, designed by Pfau Long Architecture, is flanked by vineyards and enjoys views of the Mayacamas Mountains to the west and the Vacas Mountains to the east. A quarter of the property is wooded with a mix of mature oaks, pines, redwoods, walnuts, and palms, while the remaining land is open meadow with clusters of oak trees.

Lutsko Associates worked with the architects to site the new residence and guesthouse for optimal views of the vineyards and mountains, which was important to give the house a sense of place, says associate principal Andrea Kovol.

Outdoor entertaining areas—a dining terrace, ping-pong terrace, fire-pit lounge, and pool house terrace—relate to the interiors and the views and blur the boundaries between indoors and out.

The firm consolidated the usable outdoor space by shifting the entry from a farm road that bisected the site to the far edge of the property. The graceful, meandering approach now conceals the house until the last minute, focusing instead on the woodland, where a large existing redwood is accented by flowering dogwoods and redbuds with native understory. "A sense of arrival emerges as you break out of the woodland to

The fire-pit lounge terrace embodies Napa Valley style with its clean lines and rustic accents.

Oaks punctuate the native meadow in front of the guesthouse. The planting palette, which includes *Nassella pulchra*, *Elymus glaucus*, and *Leymus triticoides*, echoes Napa Valley's naturalistic hillsides with oaks.

Right: Modern-farmhouse-inspired buildings frame the pool and gardens. Concrete seat walls create informal seating areas.

the parking court at the main house, with views to the east mountain range," says Kovol.

Thickly planted with a low-water-use Mediterranean palette and striking bands of ornamental grasses that mimic the patterns of the surrounding agrarian landscape, the property achieves a pleasing balance between cultivated and wild. Near the house, those linear patterns are echoed in the hardscaping, which is composed of alternating bands of textured paving, rectilinear stepping stones, and long, 18-inch-high seat walls that provide informal gathering places.

The guesthouse and bocce ball court sit in a native meadow that includes *Nassella pulchra* with drifts of *Elymus glaucus* and *Leymus*

triticoides. The woodland garden contains *Festuca californica* 'River House Blues', *Fragaria vesca californica*, *Iris douglasiana*, *Salvia spathacea*, and *Satureja douglasii*. Native oaks were also planted throughout the property. And swales near the vegetable beds collect water and allow it to seep back into the soil.

The result is a largely self-sustaining landscape in which native grasses are cut annually and irrigation is minimal now that the plantings are established.

Like many residential landscapes in the wine valley, lighting is limited to pathways and activity areas to preserve the night sky. The all-LED system includes downlights that create a moonlight effect on the mature trees.

Closely set native plantings surround the spa and pool house to create an intimate space.

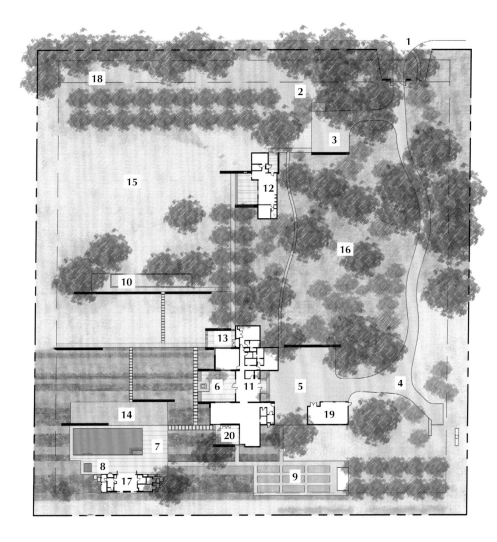

*Courtesy of
Lutsko Associates*

1	Entry gate	**8**	Spa	**15**	Native meadow
2	Fruit alley	**9**	Vegetable beds	**16**	Meadow
3	Guest parking	**10**	Bocce court	**17**	Pool house
4	Entry drive	**11**	Main house	**18**	Bioswale
5	Auto court	**12**	Guest house	**19**	Garage
6	Fire pit/lounge terrace	**13**	Ping pong terrace	**20**	Dining terrace
7	Pool terrace	**14**	Lawn		

PORTOLA VALLEY
GARDEN

PORTOLA VALLEY
LUTSKO ASSOCIATES

Drought-tolerant native California and Mediterranean plants create a transition from the built environment to the wild.

Previous page:
Four radiating concrete walls structure the landscape, delineating terraces and gardens as they gesture toward the views. *Photos: Marion Brenner*

The small guesthouse is sited below the residence and similarly tucked down into its site.

A stepped concrete path meanders toward the guesthouse
through a mix of flowering perennials and grasses. The
angled concrete wall on the left connects the main house
and guesthouse.

When San Francisco–based Feldman Architecture was commissioned to design a modestly sized, three-bedroom house and small guesthouse/studio on a 6-acre grassy hillside, the firm partnered with Lutsko Associates to develop a site plan. The owners requested a backyard terrace and a low-profile, low-water-use garden in keeping with the surrounding landscape.

With the main house nestled just below the crown of a ridge, the design team positioned the guesthouse and the garage, with its green roof, lower on the hillside. This helped the buildings blend into the land's contours and minimized grading.

Exterior spaces are defined by four landscape walls that are both obvious and understated. "Four radiating concrete walls create the framework, delineating the terraces and gardens," says Laura Jerrard, associate principal at Lutsko Associates. "The courtyard garden walls, anchored by the L-shape design of the house, fan out, expanding spaces as they gesture toward views of the greater landscape." At some points, the walls draw the eye toward the hills, and at other points they frames views.

The sloping concrete wall at the front of the house is striking as it slips through the meadow, stretching from the main house to the guesthouse. "It creates a garden enclosure without actually putting a literal enclosure in the space," Jerrard says. "It is done without blocking views or creating a visual barrier." Aesthetically, the scale and angle of the garden wall feels like a site-specific sculpture. "Sometimes it is difficult to explain the purpose of a wall like this," she says, "but the clients understood it right away."

Sea thrift and yellow yarrow flourish atop the garage's roof, blending with the larger landscape.

Left:
The staggered staircase
narrows the focus on the
entry.

Jerrard, who lectures in the College of Environmental Design at UC Berkeley, selected drought-tolerant native California and Mediterranean plants to harmonize with the existing naturalized annual grasses and create "a transition from the built environment to the wild." Plantings along the walls include Jerusalem and hummingbird sage, California fuchsia, purple needle grass, blue-eyed grass, pine muhly, and yellow and red yarrow.

The lighting plan consists simply of path lights and building-mounted fixtures, in keeping with Portola Valley's strict lighting guidelines. For their part, the owners are happy there are no bright lights interfering with their view of the hills to the west at night. Flames from the fire pit are the sole source of light at evening gatherings.

While this is a low-maintenance and low-water-usage garden, it still requires attention. Jerrard advises her clients to choose a maintenance partner who understands the design intent—someone who is detail oriented and knowledgeable about the plantings even if it is simply a matter of cutting the grasses back once a year. "One of the reasons we use straight lines and define the garden spaces clearly is so that there is a distinct line between two beds of grasses, and the gardener knows where to weed," Jerrard says.

At the front of the house, a low, sloping concrete wall slips through a meadow. The design balances the sense of openness and enclosure.

REGIONAL LANDSCAPE ARCHITECTURE

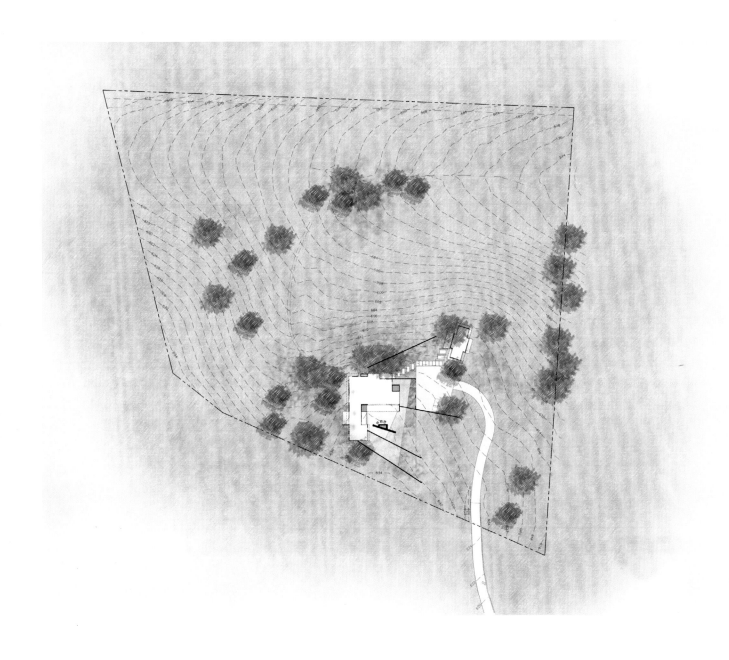

Courtesy of Lutsko Associates

STANLEY GARDEN

HEALDSBURG
ROCHE + ROCHE LANDSCAPE
ARCHITECTURE

"Most of our clients
are on private,
unmetered wells, but
we all understand we
are sipping from the
same milkshake."

—DAVID ROCHE

Previous page:
The arrival focuses on the
fountain courtyard and
forest beyond.
Photos: Marion Brenner

A board-formed concrete
wall zigzags from the
outdoor dining terrace
past the fountain to the
bocce court flanked by an
allée of *Zelkova serrata*
'Village Green'.

View from the fountain court down the entry drive toward Healdsburg.

As retirement approached, this San Francisco couple decided to build a permanent residence in Healdsburg, where they had spent weekends and holidays. The 20-acre site's vineyard and views inspired the design of their new house, a blend of craftsman, contemporary, and rural vernacular designed by architect Jeffrey Trapold. The compound, consisting of an L-shaped house, detached garage, and pair of bunkhouses, takes advantage of different vistas while providing sheltered areas, private courtyards, and gardens.

Landscape architect David Roche created "opportunities to have a direct experience of the sun, the sky, the trees, and the earth" and what he describes as "soft fascination"—a restorative, effortless awareness of the natural landscape. The scale, topography, and planting choices contribute to this awareness, he says:

"Our gardens are not about making a statement, but about creating a setting for a way of living" that is refined, yet informal and comfortable.

The local ordinance governing new construction required a minimum percentage of native plantings and a Mediterranean landscape palette, and throughout the property, plants soften and counterpoint the architecture. The crushed-gravel driveway and entry court are on axis with a small terrace containing a board-formed-concrete water feature, dwarf citrus trees, and catmint. Hedges of California wax myrtle and Grecian laurel separate the terrace and auto court, and along the breezeway between the garage and house, plane trees are underplanted with Point Reyes manzanita. A loose grove of river birch softens the rigidity of the pool courtyard, which is framed by the L-shaped residence and bunkhouses. And beyond a rolling

A sinuous line of *Betula nigra* underplanted with *Carex pansa* winds through the otherwise formal geometric design.

A long raised bed hosts a
variety of fresh vegetables
outside the potting shed.

The custom board-formed-concrete gas fire pit doubles as a table with its lift-out lid.

gate on the master bedroom wing, a private garden contains an outdoor shower and a raised, board-formed-concrete spa flanked with Quartz Creek soft rush.

A leading concern was water. "Most of our clients are on private, unmetered wells, but we all understand we are sipping from the same milkshake," Roche says. Given the area's short rainy season, the design incorporated rainwater harvesting and graywater systems, which also protect the watershed by keeping stormwater on-site. The site plan preserved as much existing vegetation as possible, given that their roots are well established and therefore need less water than new plants.

Roche's lighting philosophy is to supply just enough light to safely navigate from one point to another, and enough to read by in key areas such as an outdoor kitchen or dining terrace.

LED landscape lights are selectively placed after determining the most appropriate color temperature for a setting, and lights are often put on dimmers to soften the scene and save electricity.

A professional crew maintains this landscape on a weekly or biweekly schedule as needed. During early visits, Roche identified minor issues such as sunburn on tree trunks, which the maintenance contractor addressed with careful pruning.

"One of the things we enjoy about landscapes is that they never stop changing," he says. "As we tell our clients, it's not a couch, it isn't done the day it arrives. We encourage our clients to enjoy the growth of the landscape. Part of the joy is watching how it matures and becomes itself."

A sheltered seating nook contains *Raphiolepis umbellata* 'Minor', *Miscanthus sinensis* 'Morning Light', phormium, and a rolling gate at the spa terrace.

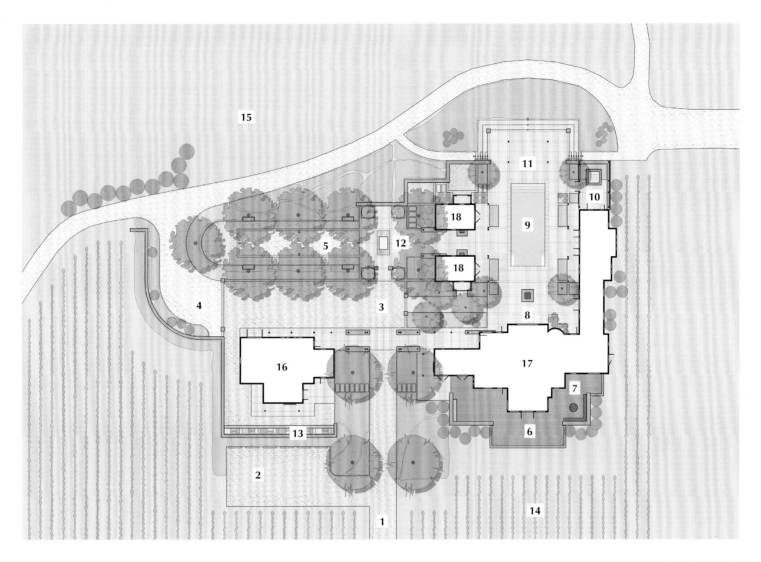

*Courtesy of Roche + Roche
Landscape Architecture*

1	Entry drive	**5**	Bocco court	**10**	Spa	**15**	Forest views
2	Guest parking	**6**	Main deck	**11**	Shade arbor	**16**	Garage
3	Auto court	**7**	Fire pit	**12**	Water feature	**17**	Main house
4	Vineyard access road	**8**	Fire feature	**13**	Vegetable garden	**18**	Guest suite
		9	Pool	**14**	Vineyard		

SONOMA VINEYARD

SONOMA
ROCHE + ROCHE LANDSCAPE
ARCHITECTURE

"We practice the mantra of unify, simplify, amplify, editing out the unnecessary and celebrating the distinctive and powerful."

—*DAVID ROCHE*

Previous page:
A Sonoma Valley view
beckons from the guest
wing terrace.
Photo: Thien Do

A linear fire feature and
stone wall anchor the
guest terrace and pool.
*Photos: Marion Brenner,
except where noted*

Right:
A gravel path from the
guest wing to the fire pit
meanders between
existing manzanitas and
rock outcroppings.

Arbutus 'Marina', *Phlomis russeliana*, and *Phormium tenax* in
a raised steel planter separate the pool and carport.

On 17 acres of steep, wooded land and volcanic rock fields that slope in every direction, the buildings in this rural compound are layered discreetly into the landscape, and hidden photovoltaic panels power the entire property, including the homeowners' electric cars. Landscape architect David Roche and his team looked for opportunities to blend the buildings with the land, which included an oak woodland with native toyons, ferns, and wildflowers.

"We pay attention to the soil, topography, previous disturbances to the site, what is currently growing—both native and introduced—solar aspects, and the areas to be landscaped intensively or passively," says Roche. "Planting design is very site specific when you pay attention to these characteristics. The land tells you what group of plants will thrive there, and you can play with that a bit."

The site elements take their cues from the house's natural cladding materials—rectilinear Montana stone and horizontal cedar siding. At the gravel driveway's entrance, boulders from the site were made into low, curving walls planted with stachys and butelaua, and the driveway loops around existing trees. "We practice the mantra of unify . . . simplify . . . amplify, editing out the unnecessary and celebrating the distinctive and powerful," Roche says.

A gravel path leads from the house to a high point, where a destination steel fire pit overlooks the scenic view and a bocce garden tucked into a gap in the rocks. This area, with its moon

garden, has become the owners' favorite spot, where the evening sun on the lichen creates a play of colors. St. Catherine's lace, matilija poppies, blue fescue, *Senecio vitalis*, finger aloe, and white rockrose accentuate the garden's grays, light greens, and whites.

Elsewhere, naturalistic sweeps of native plane trees, Point Reyes manzanita, and catmint anchor the buildings to the land. To conform to the local water-efficient-landscape ordinance,

Roche + Roche designed wood and steel "bee hotels" for native pollinator bees that live in burrows instead of hives.
Photo: Roche + Roche Landscape Architecture

the plan had to include an inventory of new and existing plantings, including size, number, and the watering needs for each, along with a drainage and irrigation plan. "Clients have to buy into the details that make a project sing, such as grading, drainage, soil preparation, and irrigation—all mostly unseen except in how they make the landscape thrive," Roche says.

The firm diversified the oak woodland plantings with additional water-wise plants such as maiden grass, New Zealand flax, and California wax myrtle. Roche selected and spaced plants to allow them to grow naturally and achieve what he calls their "genetic destiny." This approach allows for a more relaxed, natural form, reducing the need for pruning. He recommends cutting ornamental grasses annually, and evergreen grasses and grasslike relatives every other year, and fall pruning for perennials and herbs. The fruit trees are seasonally pruned, sprayed, fertilized, and harvested as part of the property's natural rhythm.

Sonoma County's dark-sky ordinance dictates downward-facing, fully shielded light fixtures. To avoid the "house of mirrors" effect at night in houses like this one with a lot of glass, Roche recommends accent lighting on tree canopies and rock faces, which adds depth to the landscape at night.

If the goal of a garden is to draw people outside, Roche's team has succeeded. "They've developed a rough trail system throughout their property to more fully engage with it," he says. "They live in a wild park!"

At the master terrace, an
existing stone outcrop forms
a backdrop to a gravel
garden with succulents.
Photo: Thien Do

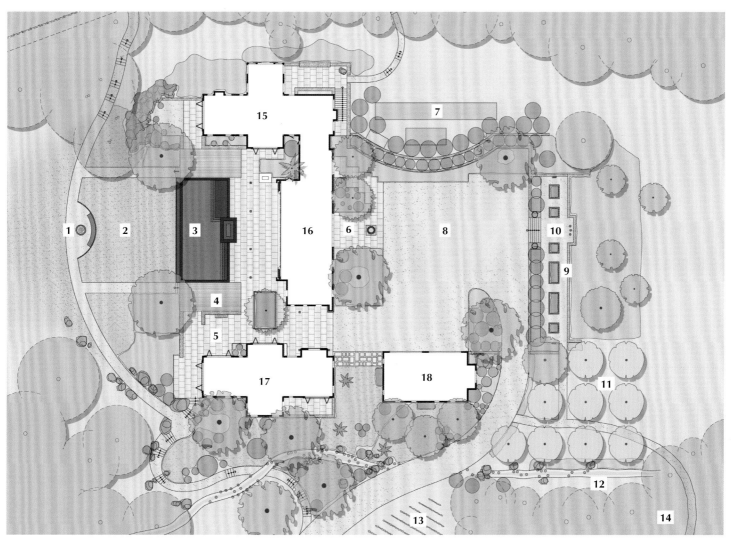

Courtesy of Roche + Roche
Landscape Architecture

1	Fire pit with steel wall	**7**	Solar panels	**13**	Vineyard
2	Native meadow	**8**	Auto court	**14**	Oak woodland
3	Pool	**9**	Vegetable garden	**15**	Master wing
4	Wood decking	**10**	Garden water feature	**16**	Great room
5	Fire feature	**11**	Orchard	**17**	Guest wing
6	Entry water feature	**12**	Seasonal draining	**18**	Garage

EDGE OF THE CONTINENT

SONOMA COAST
SHADES OF GREEN LANDSCAPE
ARCHITECTURE

"The nature on this property is amazing. You want to do something that only enhances it and makes it more useful."

—*IVE HAUGELAND*

Previous page:
The infinity pool
juxtaposed with the distant
landscape creates an
edge-of-the-continent
feeling. *Photos: Marion
Brenner*

The pool terrace holds a
variety of amenities in a
minimal footprint.

A grassy nook at the bocce court offers space for socializing or relaxing.

Shades of Green developed roughly an acre of this 25-acre property of steep, grassy hillsides with views of the nearby ocean. The original plan for an infinity pool and trellis evolved to include a guesthouse, vegetable garden, bocce ball court, fire pit, and seating areas from which to enjoy the bucolic views. "The nature on this property is amazing," says firm principal Ive Haugeland. "You just want to do something that only enhances it and makes it more useful." She developed this approach as a native of Norway, where she studied landscape architecture.

Haugeland worked with the guesthouse's architect on terracing a portion of the hillside below the main house and addressing irrigation requirements. While the planted areas are distinct from their wilder surroundings, they are designed to blend softly with the natural slope. The graded soil was reused elsewhere on the site.

Haugeland and her team selected plants that could handle the wind and salt air. Plants such as Russian sage, fountain grass, and blue oat grass were at the top of the list, since they "really celebrate the wind by the way they move," she says. Along the stairways are smaller-scale succulents and colorful flowers that people can appreciate up close. Haugeland rebalanced the existing backyard by thinning overgrown vegetation. Cypress trees were then planted along the sides and back of the house for screening.

The garden feels boundless with its soft plants that merge with the hillside.

If the pool terrace is the main attraction, the guesthouse's green roof is a charming but subtle aside. Three-inch-deep sedum mats are interspersed with grasses and other succulents to create height variations. "Part of the beauty of a green roof is that it retains water," Haugeland says, "and mats are ideal for this. They have a low saturated weight, and the green roof virtually maintains itself. The mats contain a large variety of sedums, so it's kind of a survival of the fittest. Sedums that like the exposure and fog the best will dominate."

Though Haugeland loves color, she believes that textures are equally important, and that sometimes it is necessary to limit the palette to create a thematic, focused aesthetic. Among her favorite plants is asparagus fern, a soft, fluffy bright-green plant that "looks pretty all year round and can take the spectrum of different conditions." Perennial grasses are another frequent choice, particularly blue grama, sometimes called blond ambition (as the flowers mature, they take on a blond color). "They have blond eyelashes or eyebrows—that's the flower that kind of hangs at the top of the plant." Haugeland also likes agaves and prefers *Agave attenuata* 'Variegata' for its large rosette; it is softer and not as spiny as other agaves. She's also partial to the *Aeonium arboreum* purple variety 'Black Rose', with its large rosette as a focal point.

The gracious terraces and wide landings are welcoming without competing with the house or the natural setting. Likewise, low-profile lighting consists only of downlights along pathways and the stairs and at the pool.

After the multiyear planning and construction process, the guesthouse and pool are well used, and the owners consider the property their "happiest place on earth," Haugeland says.

The soft tones of grasses and
perennials blend into the
natural landscape, while the
pool house's green roof
mimics the hills.

REGIONAL LANDSCAPE ARCHITECTURE

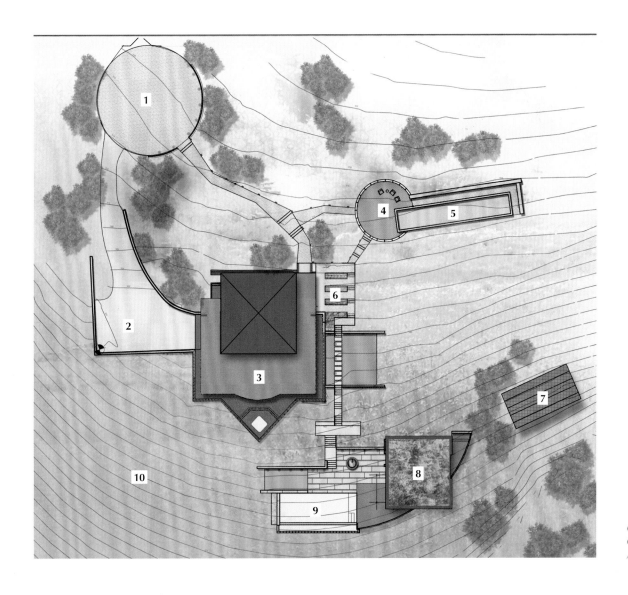

*Courtesy of Shades of
Green Landscape
Architecture*

1	Guest parking	**6**	Vegetable garden
2	Driveway	**7**	Solary array
3	House	**8**	Garage with green roof
4	Native lawn	**9**	Infinity pool
5	Bocce court	**10**	Meadow

URBAN LUXURY

SAN FRANCISCO
SHADES OF GREEN LANDSCAPE
ARCHITECTURE

Permeable paving, drought-tolerant plantings, a native lawn, rainwater harvesting, and water-efficient irrigation contributed to the property's LEED Platinum certification.

Previous page:
The terrace's graphic
paving patterns are meant
to be viewed from above.
Photos: Troon Pacific

A raised infinity lap pool
mediates the grade change
between two terraces.

"When we do gardens, we are 'exterior designers,'" says Shades of Green principal Ive Haugeland. "A garden is everything. It's not just the plants." This project is about living comfortably outdoors with amenities that extend specific interior spaces, including a kitchen and dining area. Shades of Green worked with Troon Pacific, a luxury real-estate development company, to develop the grounds of this speculative house renovation. Built in 1905 on a large city lot with views of the Golden Gate Bridge, the house is shingle-style Edwardian, but its new garden is decidedly modern in both philosophy and style. Permeable paving, drought-tolerant plantings, a native-grass lawn, rainwater harvesting, and water-wise irrigation contributed to the property's LEED Platinum certification.

Conceived as an urban oasis, the garden's bold lines and graphic materials are composed for viewing from the balconies and large windows of the home's three upper floors. The backyard was sloped and uneven, and the tradesman's alley alongside the property had been neglected. Like many homes in San Francisco, the backyard was accessed from wooden stairs, which prevented the yard from being used. To improve access, a lower floor was excavated and fitted with folding glass doors that lead directly into the garden.

The regrading allowed for a variety of outdoor living areas, including a raised, 50-foot lap pool with an infinity edge. The water sheets over the sides, where it is collected and pumped back to the pool—an effect that is soothing both visually and acoustically. The main terrace consists of dry-laid pavers with an abstract pattern of inlaid creeping thyme that slows rainwater runoff by allowing it to percolate into the ground.

Haugeland chose decomposed granite to define the dining area; she prefers the softness and informality of gravel, rock, and pebbles compared to concrete and stone. The choice of paving "depends on the client," she says. "Some people can handle the slight messiness of gravel and decomposed granite, and others cannot . . . in terms of tracking it into the house, where it can potentially scratch floors. It can get a little dusty in the summer, and muddy in the winter."

Alongside the lap pool, an ipe trellis screens the view from higher-elevation neighbors, and laurel trees line the long sides of the garden for additional privacy. A large, mature cypress tree from an adjacent yard is a focal point that adds to the garden experience. Closer to the house along the side, a contained bed of bamboo will screen the garden as it matures.

At the front of the house, five opaque glass panels, each 5 feet high, partition the small front terrace from the street. On the house side of the panels, lemons trees provide another layer of separation from the street.

Left:
Cypress trees screen the dining terrace from the neighbors.

Floor-to-ceiling folding
glass doors and large
upper-story windows open
out to emphasize
indoor-outdoor living.

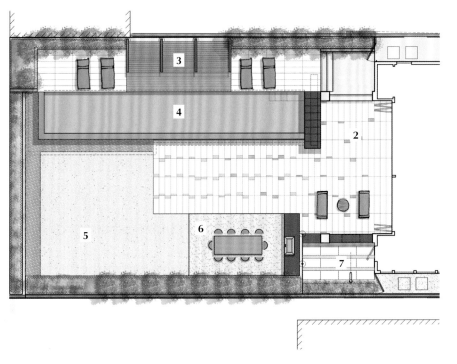

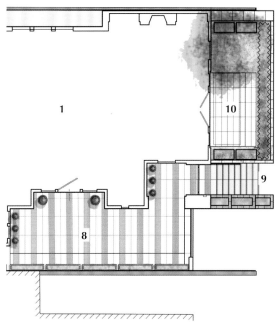

Courtesy of Shades of Green Landscape Architecture

1	House	**7**	Outdoor shower with pavers and crushed rock
2	Dry-laid pavers with groundcover	**8**	Pavers
3	Pool arbor	**9**	Front stairs
4	Pool	**10**	Balcony with rainwater storage tank below
5	Lawn		
6	Crushed rock		

TANK HILL

SAN FRANCISCO
SURFACEDESIGN

As cities densify, the value of open space increases, both psychologically and financially.

Previous page:
A modernist courtyard garden offers a serene break from the city, extending domestic life beyond the home's walls.
Photos: Marion Brenner

In contrast to the inward-looking courtyard, the roof deck gazes out on panoramic views. Custom-milled ipe wood planters and benches frame a silver garden.

Architectural planes
explore the qualities of
wood, basalt, and
limestone.

To avoid building another story on their midcentury home, which would block the neighbors' views, the owners took the approach of many other San Franciscans who want more square footage: they went down instead of up, carving a new floor from under the house. The down-to-the-studs redesign left the owners with very little backyard, which was hemmed in by a precipitous slope leading to Tank Hill, a hilltop park in the Cole Valley neighborhood. What's more, a retaining wall was needed to hold back the slope, further reducing the opportunity for plantings.

The owners didn't mind, since they were seeking a resilient and easy-upkeep courtyard rather than a cultivated garden. Inspired by the vertical, cliff-like edge, Surfacedesign principals James Lord and Roderick Wyllie developed a solution that is both practical and poetic—a retaining wall that could double as a climbing wall, since the owners are avid rock climbers.

Holding back the slope are two offset concrete walls clad in split-faced basalt panels in varying thicknesses; they create a bas relief pattern with nooks and crannies that the owners can scale. A second tall fireplace wall clad in limestone features an appealing pattern of protruding limestone blocks that double as handholds and footholds. Wyllie remarks, "The texture of these materials was inspired by the carving of the earth, which in many ways defines the space. That sense of weight and ruggedness is something we see in grotto gardens and historic Italian gardens such as the Villa Giulia."

Limestone pavers are interplanted with Irish moss and mondo grass. Lights and fire accentuate the stone hearth and wood feature wall.

The paving consists of a rhythmic, staggered pattern of limestone interplanted with Irish moss and mondo grass. A variety of Japanese maples highlight the striking differences in each tree's color and leaf shape. Cubed ceramic stools by Atelier Vierkant in Belgium, which also made the planters, provides seating in front of the linear fireplace.

On the opposite side of the courtyard are lightweight aluminum tables designed by Christian Woo, and an L-shaped bench made of the same material as the basalt rock wall services the grilling area. At night, recessed LEDs highlight the hearth and limestone wall niches.

The outdoor experience continues up on the roof deck, where a blackened-steel fire pit and custom-milled ipe wood planters contain *Agave attenuata* 'Nova', dudleya succulents, *Echeveria colorata*, *Helichrysum petiolare*, *Artemesia schmidtiana*, and *Thymus argenteus*. The roof deck's uninterrupted views of the city and bay are a contrast to the more intimate courtyard below. As cities densify, Wyllie says, the value of open space increases, both psychologically and financially.

The hearth is an abstract
composition of limestone
and blackened steel.

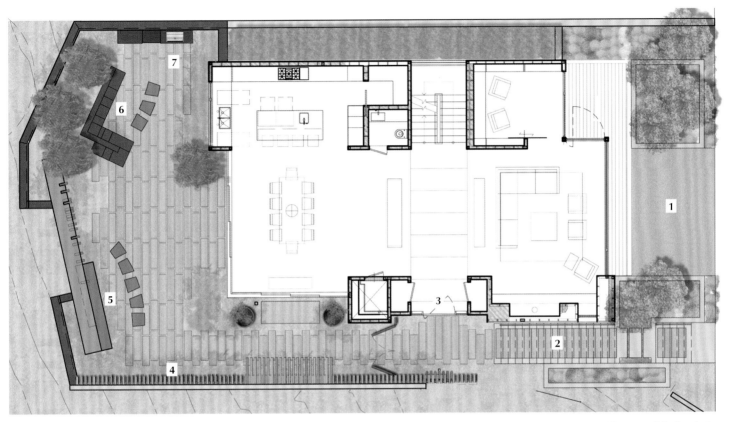

Courtesy of Surfacedesign

1	Driveway	**5**	Hearth wall
2	Entrance steps	**6**	Stone bench
3	Front door	**7**	Outdoor kitchen
4	Wood feature wall		

BUTTERFLY HOUSE

SAN FRANCISCO
SURFACEDESIGN

Japanese *tsubo-niwa* courtyard gardens are often small and enclosed; the goal is to bring nature into the house, both symbolically and literally.

Previous page:
Sliding pocket doors
seamlessly connect the
interior with the garden,
where woolly thyme
softens the paving joints.
Japanese anemone and
western swordfern
enhance the floating
appearance of the
cantilevered concrete
planes. *Photos: Marion
Brenner, except where
noted*

Recessed lighting
enhances the garden's
intimacy by highlighting its
floating architectural
edges.

This 1953 home in Russian Hill combines the original two units and studio apartment into a single-family home with panoramic views of the Golden Gate Bridge and Alcatraz. The new floor plan incorporated the owners' art collection, in particular a sculpture commissioned from artist Paul Villinski for the wall of the three-story foyer. Villinski, known for his series of butterfly sculptures, created a large group of upward-flying blue butterflies, which led to the name Butterfly House.

As a counterpoint to the city's views, lights, and sounds, the owners wanted an inward-looking garden—a tranquil and intimate space where they could connect with nature. Surfacedesign proposed a Japanese *tsubo-niwa* courtyard. These gardens are often small and enclosed, and the goal is to bring nature into the house, both symbolically and literally.

A set of horizontal planes defines two courtyard levels—a concrete perimeter walkway on grade with the garage, and a sunken courtyard garden sitting level with the house entrance. Elegant limestone steps connect the two levels.

The lower garden is accessed from the living room through a wall of sliding glass pocket doors. Woolly thyme softens the paving joints, while Japanese anemone and western swordfern outline the garden and enhance the floating appearance of the cantilevered concrete planes that enclose it on three sides. In large pots are succulents, including Mexican Giant echeveria, blue foxtail agave, and hen and chicks.

The focal point is a hearth that integrates a water fountain and screens the deck stairs. "It's an abstract composition of pristine white concrete and the rippling surface of a black-basalt fountain wall that slides behind the flame of the linear fire pit," Wyllie says. "It invokes the forces of nature, and the afternoon winds from the San Francisco Bay dematerialize in the courtyard as leaves and petals dance across the base of the fireplace."

For the courtyard walkway from the garage, Surfacedesign partnered with the foundry Blue Barn Arts on the design of a cast-aluminum hanging sculpture made of butterfly-size cranes. The sculpture's gentle kinetic movement and reflections cause the cranes to shimmer in a tall, ethereal column beneath an opening in the deck above. A misty, fog-like water feature enhances the effect.

Key lighting comes from an LED light wash on the basalt panels inside the fireplace, which is more dramatic when the fire and water feature are in use. Recessed LED strips line the limestone steps into the garden and the underside of the

concrete hearth and bench seating. Away from the fireplace, an uplight on the magnolia tree produces a dramatic figure. With its large windows, the house also acts as a garden lantern at night.

"The landscape is a true connection to their living spaces on every level of the house, providing new vantage points to engage with the city around them," Wyllie says.

A cast-aluminum crane sculpture reflects sunlight from an opening in the deck and is lit from below in the evening. A misting feature highlights its presence as a visual terminus for the portico.
Photos: Marion Brenner

Right:
The courtyard garden is a respite carved out of the dense urban setting.

Limestone stairs connect the floating concrete walkway to the limestone patio and bridge the level change between the garage and family entrance.

1 Crane water feature
2 Garden steps
3 Sunken garden
4 Hearth feature wall
5 Pivot gate

Courtesy of Surfacedesign

RANDALL GARDEN

SAN FRANCISCO
TERREMOTO

"When you need to value-engineer things, you get to the essence of the design. You kind of peel away what you don't need."

—*ALAIN PEAUROI*

Previous page:
The fire pit is a beacon at
the back of the garden,
drawing family and friends
outdoors in the evening.
Photos: Bruce Damonte

A deck becomes a bench
becomes a fence. The
unstained cedar will
weather to a beautiful
silvery gray.

Before the owners rebuilt their home, the backyard was overgrown, sloped, and nearly unusable. For the landscape redesign, they wanted a flat yard they could access directly from the house. They imagined dining outdoors and relaxing around a fire pit, and they wanted to preserve an apple tree their children enjoyed picking from. In addition to an olive tree, the owners requested an edible garden their children could help tend.

Terremoto, a landscape architecture firm founded by David Godshall and Alain Peauroi, excavated a sizeable area of the yard to create a flat entry from the house. Perhaps the most striking landscape feature is the angled, decomposed granite walkway that breaks up the geometry's formality. The diagonal slash incorporates steps with Corten steel treads and traverses two terraced vegetable beds, ending at the fire pit terrace at the rear.

The slash is part of a throughway from the front to back of the property. "The house is very open, so when you have the front doors and back doors open, it should feel like one space as you transition through the house, from one part of the landscape to another," says Peauroi.

The designers selected a minimal, blue-gray plant palette for its simplicity and quiet aesthetic. "Atlas fescue is an awesome grass we like to use, though it is not native to California," says Godshall, who oversees the firm's Los Angeles office. "We were introduced to it in *The American Meadow Garden* by John Greenlee, a book that has had a huge impact in our office." Other plantings included a variety of succulents such as giant chalk dudleya.

On hilly San Francisco streets, neighbors often share a retaining wall to hold back the grade change between properties. In this case, one of the 10-foot-high shared walls was cleverly redesigned to incorporate a bench.

This project exemplifies another principle that underpins California's history of modern design, which is to distill a design to its purest form. "We had designed much more decking, but due

Edible garden beds aren't
far from the kitchen.

A boardwalk bisects a minimalist meadow. Corten steel fins strike lines along the walk.

to cost we had to cut back," Peauroi says. "It actually worked out better. When you need to value-engineer things, you get to the essence of the design. You kind of peel away what you don't need."

To keep the lighting subtle along pathways, Terremoto often specifies thin, sticklike LED fixtures that almost disappear. "On this project the fixtures are little higher and more prominent, but we tried to place them where plantings grow, and maybe they get hidden over time as

plants get larger," notes Peauroi. Hanging festoon lights provide a soft accent.

"The clients now spend more time outside than inside," he says. "They cannot help but enjoy the yard from the kitchen; even when the large glass doors are closed you see the yard."

This very low-maintenance garden requires only about an hour of work per month to keep it tidy, and the Atlas fescue grasses are cut back annually.

At sunset the garden turns silvery, and lighting gives it form when viewed from the second story.

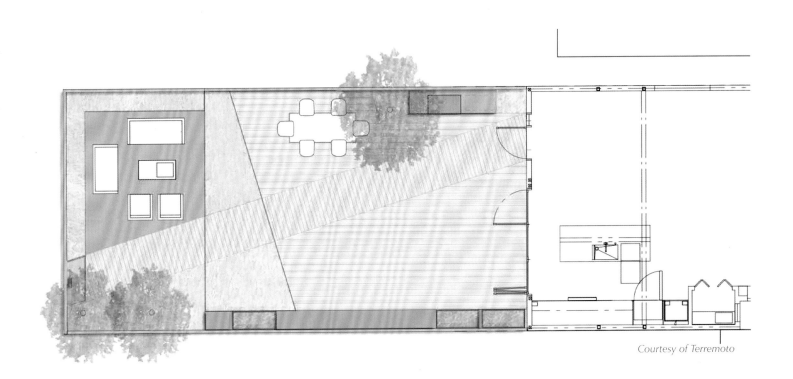

Courtesy of Terremoto

DENMARK GARDEN

SONOMA
TERREMOTO

Boulders from a local
materials yard were
used for seating—
another way to execute
a simple design that is
not overly detailed.

A simple cedar fence feels appropriate in this rural setting and creates privacy along the street edge. An existing redwood tree towers just inside the property line. *Photos: Caitlin Atkinson*

An edible garden bed near
the kitchen keeps herbs
close at hand.

A simple architectural feature can be a key organizing principle outdoors. An example is this weekend home set amid Sonoma's grassy hills, where a ribbon of unstained cedar boardwalk gives the family a new lease on outdoor living. When the owners finished renovating their weekend home, they began looking for ways to screen the road, create outdoor spaces for entertaining, and enhance the pool and spa area.

Terremoto devised a series of spaces linked by a low-key boardwalk that connects the front and back yards while minimizing damage to the roots of existing redwoods and a specimen Japanese maple. At the front of the property, an unstained cedar fence hints at the experience to come. The boardwalk begins at the front gate, leading to the front door over a swath of decomposed granite and Atlas fescue before bending around to the back of the house, where it forms a raised terrace overlooking the concrete-framed pool and spa.

While the owners wanted a wood pool deck, it "seemed like too much wood to us, so we went with concrete," which also defines the pool as a separate element, says landscape architect Alain Peauroi. "Another factor was weather. Wet wood around the deck does not have the same longevity as concrete."

Inspired by the surrounding grass hills, Peauroi designed a decomposed granite terrace and Corten steel fire pit in the septic area at the back of the property, repeating the tufts of Atlas fescue that occur around the property. Boulders from a local materials yard were used for seating—another way to execute a simple design that is not overly detailed. "The clients were surprisingly open to the rock seating," he says. "They thought it would be fun to have parties with people sitting on the rocks."

A Swan Hill olive hedgerow screens the house from the road, and the existing Marina strawberry trees, which were not getting enough sunlight, were moved to the rear of the property, where they now thrive. And a barbecue grill, bocce ball court framed in Corten steel, and two raised vegetable planters sit close to the kitchen for easy access.

Nighttime illumination consists of simple LED path lights and festoon lights at the bocce ball court, while gooseneck barn lights mounted to the house along the boardwalk lend a farmhouse feeling.

Most of the site is permeable, since water drains through the decomposed granite. The Atlas fescue does not need to be cut, but dead growth gets raked out occasionally with a handheld cultivator. The low-water-use landscape is ideal for a second home. "We try to approach all our projects, including this one, with zero-maintenance, even though there's no such thing," Peauroi says. "When you come up for the weekend, you just want to enjoy the property."

Boulders encircle a steel fire ring within a meadow of silvery grasses and decomposed granite. The space is unconventional and tranquil.

The boardwalk's directionality highlights the scale contrast between the redwood and Japanese maple.

Courtesy of Terremoto

1	Driveway
2	Raised cedar decking
3	Bocce court
4	Raised vegetable beds
5	Outdoor kitchen
6	Fire pit
7	Native grass meadow and accent grasses

RESOURCES

Church, Thomas Dolliver. *Gardens Are for People: How to Plan for Outdoor Living.* New York: Reinhold, 1955.

DiLiLAH: Digital Library of Landscape Architecture History. www.dililah.org

Eckbo, Garrett. *Landscape for Living.* New York: Dodge, 1950.

Greenlee, John. *The American Meadow Garden: Creating a Natural Alternative to the Traditional Lawn.* Portland, OR: Timber Press, 2009.

Halprin, Lawrence. "How Far Can Naturalism Go in a Garden?" *House Beautiful*, May 1948: 163.

Van Atta, Susan, and Peter Gaede. *The Southern California Native Flower Garden: A Guide to Size, Bloom, Foliage, Color and Texture.* Layton, UT: Gibbs Smith, 2009.

DESIGNERS

BaDesign
Oakland, California
www.landlinelandscape.com

Bionic
San Francisco, California
www.bioniclandscape.com

Einwiller Kuehl
Oakland, California
www.einwillerkuehl.com

KSA Design Studio
Marina del Rey, California
www.ksadesignstudio.com

Lutsko Associates
San Francisco, California
www.lutskoassociates.com

Roche + Roche Landscape Architecture
Sonoma, California
www.rocheandroche.com

Shades of Green Landscape Architecture
Sausalito, California
www.shadesofgreenla.com

Surface Design
San Francisco, California
www.sdisf.com

Terremoto
Los Angeles, California
www.terremoto.la

ACKNOWLEDGMENTS

When I initially started researching projects and firms in the Bay Area, I had conversations with Sarah Kuehl, of Einwiller Kuehl. She mentioned people such as Marta Kephart, and other projects I had not yet discovered. Sarah's open nature, absent of ego and competitiveness, gave me my first sense of how respectful and collegial landscape architects are among themselves.

I appreciate how Marcel Wilson of Bionic expanded my perceptions in unexpected ways, especially when we spoke about the architecture of complexity. Laura Jerrard of Lutsko Associates also provided additional insight for my own edification.

Special thanks to Marta Kephart, vice president and COO of Rana Creek Design. You are a contributor, participant, and witness to the evolution and importance of thoughtful design. Your insights are an affirmation of your commitment and passion for landscape architecture and the environment. The level of involvement and attention I received from all the firms was wonderful. Thank you for your generosity and support. Your staffs and representatives were equally kind: Angelika Williams, Anthony Stinson, Bradley Kraushaar, Cat Grey, Jacqueline Darjes, John van Duyl, Judith Yang, Michal Kapitulnik, and Wenpei Wang.

I am especially grateful to photographers Art Gray, Bruce Damonte, Caitlin Atkinson, Keith Baker, Matthew Millman, Nic Lehoux, Steve Lacap, and Thien Do. Your photography serves as a visual record but, even more so, speaks to the fine-art aspects of landscape architecture photography. This is uniquely true of Marion Brenner, whose photography is largely featured in the book. As the leading Bay Area landscape photographer, I see Marion's work with equal significance as photographers Julius Shulman and Barbara Morgan. Although their subject matter is different, the cultural and intrinsic values are a parallel.

My writing this book was made possible by Cheryl Weber, senior editor with Schiffer Publishing. Cheryl advocated for this series of landscape architecture books and my involvement. It is an honor for me to write the first books in the series. Thank you, Cheryl.

My personal thanks to Yolanda Lopez-Head and Robin Intemann. I am a beneficiary of your experience and guidance. Janet Tani, I appreciate our long friendship and your encouragement. Larry Norman, thank you for helping me reduce NASs, among other things.

Olga, my heartfelt thanks.